MAKING SCIENCE WORK

Weighing
and
Measuring

TERRY JENNINGS

Illustrations by
Peter Smith and
Catherine Ward

RSVP
RAINTREE
STECK-VAUGHN
PUBLISHERS
The Steck-Vaughn Company

Austin, Texas

Published by Raintree Steck-Vaughn Publishers, an imprint of Steck-Vaughn Company

A Mirabel Book

Produced by Cynthia Parzych Publishing, Inc.
648 Broadway, New York, NY 10012

Designed by Arcadia Consultants

Printed and bound in Spain by International Graphic Service

1 2 3 4 5 6 7 8 9 0 pl 99 98 97 96 95

Library of Congress Cataloging-in-Publication Data
Jennings, Terry J.
    Weighing and measuring / Terry Jennings / Illustrations by Peter Smith and Catherine
      Ward.
      p. cm. — (Making science work)
    Includes index.
    ISBN 0–8172–3963–4
    ISBN 0–8172–4256–2 (softcover)
    1. Scales (Weighing instruments)—Juvenile literature.
  2. Measuring instruments—Juvenile literature. [1. Weights and measures.] I. Smith, Peter,
  1948– ill. II. Ward, Catherine, ill. III. Title. IV. Series: Jennings, Terry J. Making science work.
    QC107.J395 1996
    681'.2—dc20
                                         95–4737
                                               CIP
                                             AC

PHOTO CREDITS
Art Directors Photo Library: 20 left, 20 right (© Kord),
21 bottom, 28 top
B & U International Picture Service: 12 bottom,
28 bottom
Cosworth Engineering: 12 top
Cutts, Paddy: 6
© Jonathon Eastland: 25
Jennings, Dr Terry: 24 top and bottom
Science & Society Picture Library: 21 top

Key to Symbols

 "See for Yourself" element

 Demonstrates the principles of the subject

 Warning! Adult help is required

 Activity for the child to try

Contents

People Weigh and Measure

People use many different kinds of tools. Many people try to discover new things. Some people make new inventions. Others check that machines and materials are safe and working well. To do these things, people measure. Scientists often make graphs and charts to show what they find. This helps people understand what they have discovered.

This book looks at some of the things people weigh and measure. It tells you how weighing and measuring tools work.

A weatherman measuring temperature

A coach timing runners

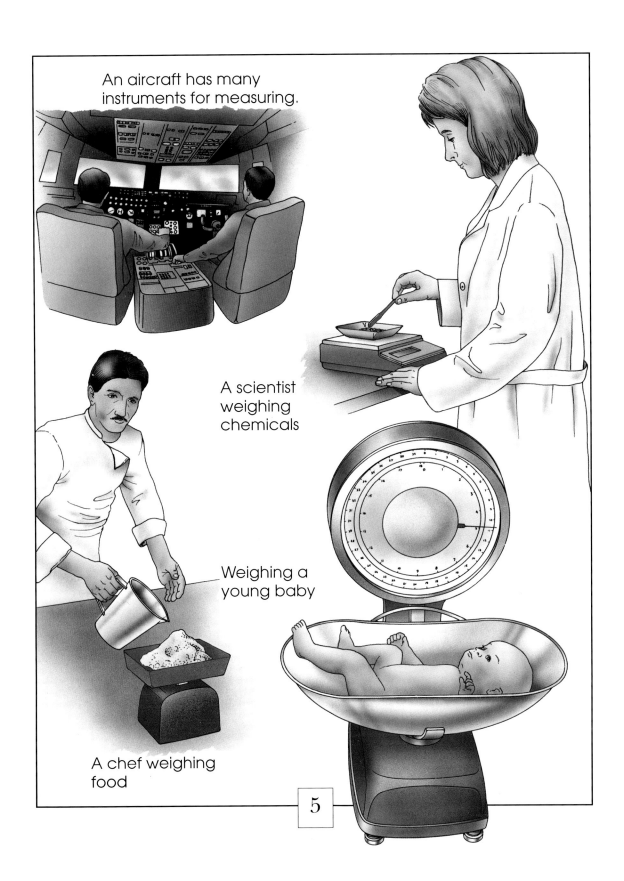

An aircraft has many instruments for measuring.

A scientist weighing chemicals

Weighing a young baby

A chef weighing food

5

Everyday Weighing and Measuring
See for Yourself

Everyone needs to weigh and measure. Long ago people measured the length of things with their feet, hands, or arms. They weighed things with grains of wheat or stones.

Measure and weigh some things using your hands or stones. Compare your results with those of your friends.

Can you see why today we have set measurements? These set measurements are called standard measurements. Feet and inches, meters and centimeters, pounds and ounces, and kilograms and grams are examples of standard measurements. These measurements are the same all over the world.

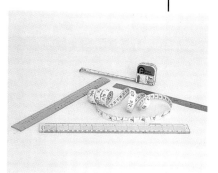

Today we use these things to measure.

6

Using feet to measure

Using arms to measure

Using fingers to measure

7

The Earth pulls everything down toward its center. This pull of the Earth is called gravity. The weight of something is how much gravity is pulling on it.

This weighing tool is called a spring scale. It has a spring inside it. When you hang something on the hook, the spring stretches. The heavier the object, the more the spring stretches. You can read the weight of the object on the scale.

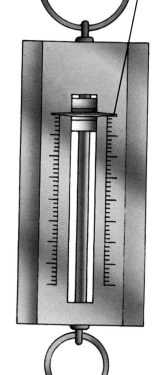

Pointer on scale shows weight

Object on hook stretches spring

Using a spring scale

This weighing tool also has a spring. This time the spring is pressed down or squashed. The heavier the object, the more the spring is squashed. As the spring is squashed, the needle on the scale moves.

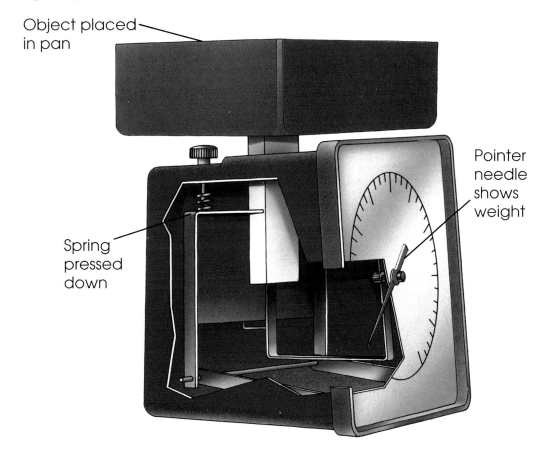

Object placed in pan

Spring pressed down

Pointer needle shows weight

Using a top pan spring balance

Weighing – See for Yourself

1 Tape ruler

Tape

Ruler

Tape

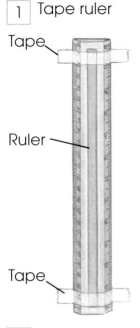

Make a spring scale. Tape a ruler to the wall. Attach a strong rubber band to a paper clip. Tack the paper clip to the wall above the ruler. Make holes around the edges of a paper cup. Hang the paper cup from the rubber band using string. Put small weights in the cup one at a time. Mark where the bottom of the cup comes to on the ruler scale.

2 Attach rubber band to paper clip

Paper clip

Rubber band

3 Tack paper clip to wall

Paper clip

Tack

4 Put string through holes in paper cup and hang

String

Holes

Cup

5 Put small weights in cup

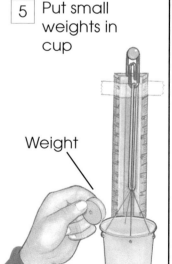

Weight

Cup

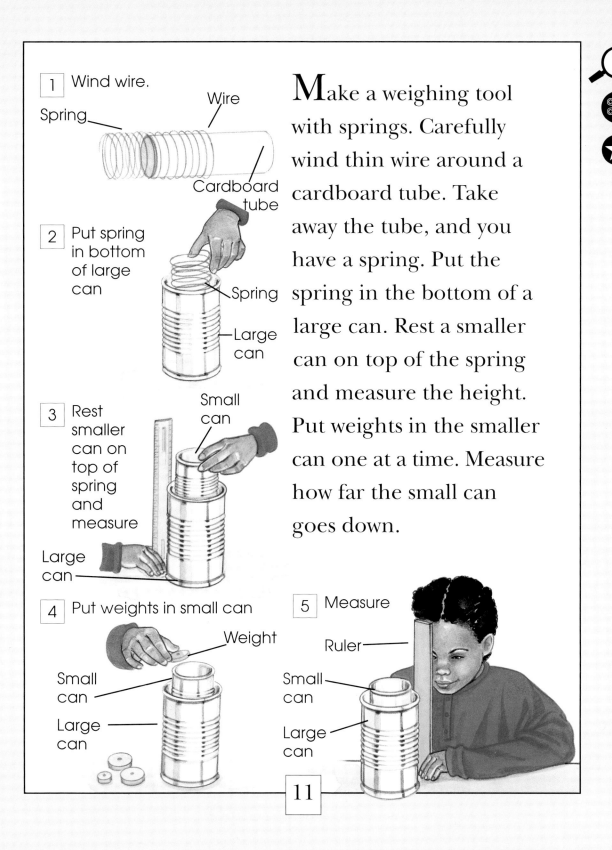

1 Wind wire.

Spring

Wire

Cardboard tube

2 Put spring in bottom of large can

Spring

Large can

3 Rest smaller can on top of spring and measure

Small can

Large can

4 Put weights in small can

Weight

Small can

Large can

5 Measure

Ruler

Small can

Large can

Make a weighing tool with springs. Carefully wind thin wire around a cardboard tube. Take away the tube, and you have a spring. Put the spring in the bottom of a large can. Rest a smaller can on top of the spring and measure the height. Put weights in the smaller can one at a time. Measure how far the small can goes down.

11

Measuring Exactly

Some people need to measure very carefully. This car part fits in the engine. It has to be exactly the right size. If it is not, the engine will not work properly.

Measuring a car part.

Parts of a watch need to be measured exactly, too. They cannot be too large or too small. If they are, the watch will not work. These parts are measured with a micrometer.

A watchmaker must measure exactly.

Scientists and engineers measure accurately with a micrometer. An object is placed in the micrometer. The screw in the handle is turned until it will not turn anymore. The micrometer's scale shows how thick the object is.

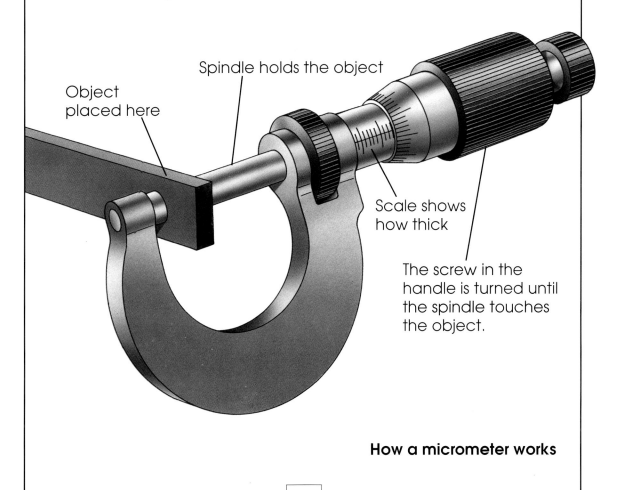

Object placed here

Spindle holds the object

Scale shows how thick

The screw in the handle is turned until the spindle touches the object.

How a micrometer works

Measuring Small Objects
See for Yourself

You can measure how small objects are. You need two blocks of wood and a ruler. Put a small object, such as a dried pea or bean, on the table. Put a piece of wood on each side of the pea or bean. Measure the space between the pieces of wood with the ruler.

Ruler

Wood

Bean

It is difficult to measure very small objects.
You can use tweezers.

Put a radish seed next to the scale on a ruler. Use a
magnifying glass to see exactly how wide the seed is.
Compare the size of the radish seed to the size of
the pea you measured before.

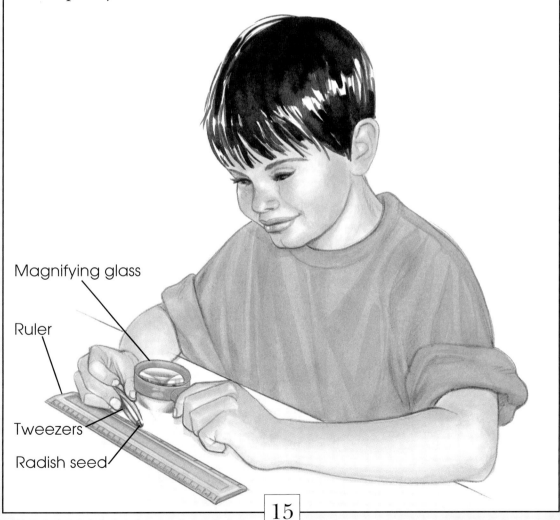

Magnifying glass

Ruler

Tweezers

Radish seed

Measuring Long Distances

Sometimes we want to measure long distances. We could not, for example, use a tape measure to see how far away the moon is. One way to do it is to use a laser.

A laser sends out a powerful beam of light. When astronauts went to the moon, they left behind a large mirror. A laser beam bounces or reflects off the mirror. The beam of light then comes back to Earth. Scientists measure how long it takes for the light to go to the moon and then back to Earth. They can use math to work out how far away the moon is.

Scientists send out laser beam

Earth as seen from the moon

Beam of light comes back to Earth

How a laser is used to measure long distances

The Earth is larger than the moon. Viewed from the moon the Earth looks like it is smaller.

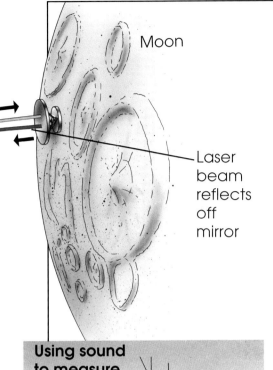

Moon

Laser beam reflects off mirror

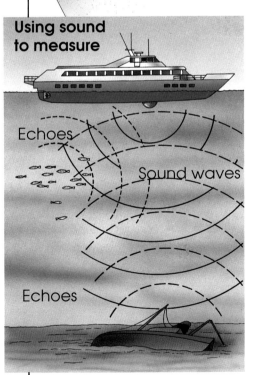

Using sound to measure

Echoes

Sound waves

Echoes

Scientists and sailors need to know how deep the ocean is. A machine on the bottom of a ship sends out small bursts of sound. The sound goes down to the bottom of the ocean. It bounces off the bottom, off schools of fish, or off a wrecked ship. It then comes back as an echo. If the echo comes back quickly, the sounds and their echoes have traveled a short distance. If the echo takes a long time to come back, the sounds have traveled a great distance. An instrument on the ship measures how far the sounds travel.

Sometimes we do not need to measure. We can estimate instead. That means you can make a careful guess of the size or weight of something. You might estimate how far you have gone on a long walk or bicycle ride. You might estimate how high a wall or fence is. Try estimating how wide a room is. Write down your estimate. Then measure the room. How close was your estimate?

Estimating how high a tree is

3-foot
(1-m)
stick

This is one way to estimate the height of a tree. Ask a friend to hold a stick 3 feet (1 m) long under the tree. Stand away from the tree. Hold your arm straight out with a pencil in front of you. Move your thumb until a piece of the pencil above your thumb looks as high as the stick. Stay in the same place. Now see how many pieces of the pencil it takes to measure the height of the tree. If it takes six lengths, then the tree is six times three or 18 feet (6 m) high. Estimate the height of a tall building in the same way.

People have always been interested in measuring time. There are two natural units of time that we use. A day is the time the Earth takes to spin around once. A year is the time the Earth takes to travel once around the sun.

Clocks were invented to measure time. A sundial uses a moving shadow to measure time. The shadow moves as the Earth turns and the sun seems to move across the sky. An hourglass uses the flow of sand to measure time.

A sundial

An hourglass

Some clocks use a swinging pendulum. A pendulum is a weight on a string or piece of wire. Each swing of the pendulum takes exactly the same time. In some clocks the power to move the pendulum comes from a wound-up spring. In other clocks the pendulum is moved by a weight that slowly pulls a string down.

A pendulum

Today many clocks and watches use quartz. A piece of quartz can vibrate quickly. Each vibration takes exactly the same time. These clocks and watches get their power from small batteries.

A quartz watch

1 Nail wood.

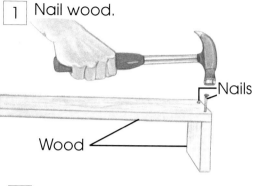

Nails

Wood

A water clock uses the flow of water to measure time. To make a water clock, ask an adult to nail two pieces of wood together. You also need four plastic cups. Make a small hole in the bottom of three cups with a tack. Tack the cups to the wood. Fill the top cup with water. How long does it take for all the water to reach the bottom cup?

2 Make hole in cup with tack

Cup

Tack

3 Tack cups

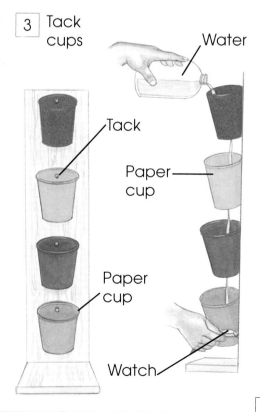

Water

Tack

Paper cup

Paper cup

Watch

4 Fill the top cup with water and time the water.

1 Cut bottom off bottle

Bottle

2 Make marks on jar

Jar

1 inch (3 cm) marks

3 Turn bottle upside down and fill with sand

Bottle

Jar

Scale

4 Time the sand.

Bottle

Jar

Sand

Scale

Make a sand clock. Ask an adult to cut the bottom off a clean soft drink bottle. Make some marks 1 inch (3 cm) apart on the side of a jar. Put the bottle in the jar upside down. Fill the bottle with dry sand. Time how long it takes for the sand to reach each of the marks. Use your sand clock to time how long you take to read a page of this book.

There is a thick blanket of air around the Earth. As we move away from the ground, there is less air. There is no air at all in space.

Air presses on everything. When the weather is about to change, the air pressure changes. This air pressure can be measured using an instrument called a barometer. Barometers help people to predict the weather.

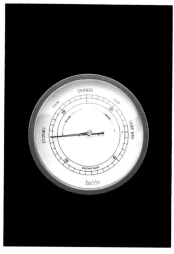

Low pressure can mean stormy weather.

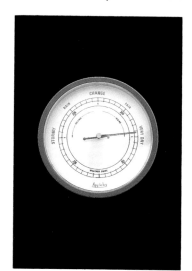

High pressure can mean dry weather.

This barometer contains a box made of metal. There is no air in the box. When the air pressure becomes lower, the box gets bigger. When the air pressure becomes higher, the box is squeezed or becomes smaller. A needle moves when the size of the box changes.

Metal box changes

Pointer needle shows pressure

Scale

An aneroid barometer

Air Pressure and Barometers
See for Yourself

Air pushes against things all the time. You can see what happens when air pressure changes. Drink all the juice out of a small juice box with a straw. Keep on sucking the air out of the box. Watch what happens. As the box empties, the air outside the box pushes the sides of the box in.

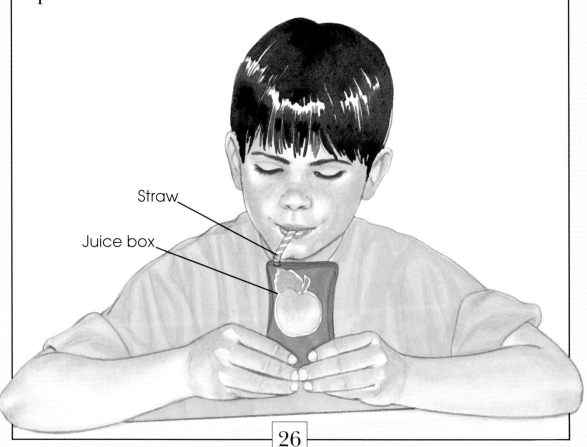

Straw

Juice box

Blow into the box. Watch the box as the air rushes into it. Adding air pushes the sides of the box back out.

Straw

Juice box

Temperature and Thermometers

Sometimes we need to know exactly how hot or cold things are. To do that we measure the temperature. Thermometers are used to measure temperature. They are made of glass. The bulb and the bottom of the tube are filled with mercury or colored alcohol.

A clinical thermometer

On a warm day the mercury or colored alcohol gets hotter. It climbs higher up the tube. The higher it climbs, the higher the temperature. On a cool day the mercury or colored alcohol cools. It moves down the tube. The lower the mercury or colored alcohol moves down the tube, the lower the temperature.

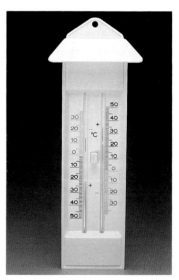

A maximum and minimum thermometer

Not all thermometers have liquid in them. This oven thermometer has two strips of metal. When the strips of metal are heated, they get longer. One gets longer than the other. As the strips get longer, they bend. When they bend, they move the needle. As the strips cool, they straighten out. This moves the needle the other way.

Temperature gauge shows how hot it is inside the oven

Metal tube connects probe to thermometer

Metal strip bends

Probe inside oven conducts heat to metal strip

How an oven thermometer works

Make your own thermometer. Pour cold water into a clear plastic bottle. Stop when it is half full. Add two or three drops of food coloring. Put a drinking straw in the bottle. Make sure the straw is in the water. Seal the opening of the bottle with modeling clay. Blow gently down the straw. The water will rise a little way up the straw. Mark on the straw where the water level is. Put the bottle in warm water. What happens to the water in the straw? Put the bottle in cold water. What happens now?

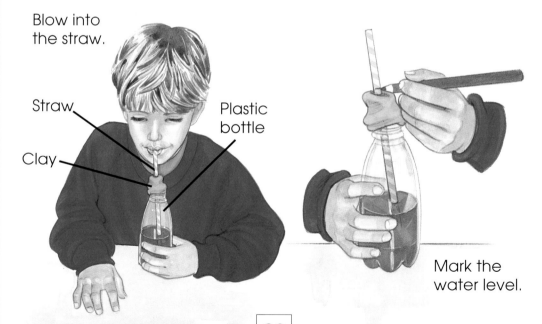

Blow into the straw.

Straw

Clay

Plastic bottle

Mark the water level.